# CONTEN

GU00356856

# Poetry Book Society

| | |
|---|---|
| CHOICE RECOMMENDATION SPECIAL COMMENDATION SELECTORS | SANDEEP PARMAR & VIDYAN RAVINTHIRAN |
| TRANSLATION SELECTOR | GEORGE SZIRTES |
| PAMPHLET SELECTORS | A.B. JACKSON & DEGNA STONE |
| WILD CARD SELECTOR | ANTHONY ANAXAGOROU |
| CONTRIBUTORS | SOPHIE O'NEILL NATHANIEL SPAIN EMILY TATE |
| EDITORIAL & DESIGN | ALICE KATE MULLEN |

**Membership Options**

**Associate** 4 *Bulletins* a year (UK £22, Europe £35, Rest of the World £42)
**Full** 4 Choice books and 4 *Bulletins* a year (£55, £65, £75)
**Charter** 20 books and 4 *Bulletins* (£180, £210, £235)
**Education** 4 books, 4 *Bulletins*, posters, teaching notes (£79, £89, £99)
**Charter Education** 20 books, 4 *Bulletins*, posters, teaching notes (£209, £245, £275)
**Translation** 4 Translation books and 4 *Bulletins* (£65, £90, £99)
**Student** 4 Choice books and 4 *Bulletins* (£35, £55, £65)
**Translation Plus Full** 4 Choices, 4 *Bulletins* & 4 Translation books (£98, £120, £132)
**Translation Plus Charter** 20 books, 4 *Bulletins* & 4 Translation books (£223, £265, £292)
**Single copies** £6
**Cover Art** Ivan Lindsay www.juvan-arts.com

Supported using public funding by
**ARTS COUNCIL ENGLAND**

Poetry Book Society | Churchill House | 12 Mosley Street |
Newcastle upon Tyne | NE1 1DE | 0191 230 8100 | pbs@inpressbooks.co.uk

WWW.POETRYBOOKS.CO.UK

# LETTER FROM THE PBS

Time flies. We have now been running the PBS for over two years and I thought I would take this letter as an opportunity to thank you, our members, for your continued support. We love our work supporting contemporary poetry and feel honoured to be in this position of recommending new and forthcoming works, a role we and our poet selectors take incredibly seriously.

We are beginning to grow the number of events we are involved in, from sponsoring readings at festivals to running our own *Bulletin* launch events, which we see as an opportunity to meet and speak to our members face to face. Thanks to everyone who came along to our Summer Showcase at the Southbank Centre, our Ledbury Poetry Festival stall and the Northern Poetry Symposium at Newcastle Poetry Festival. We will be at the Free Verse Poetry Book Fair in London on the 22nd September and supporting a Winchester Poetry Festival event on the 6th October with Vahni Capildeo. Please save the date for our Winter *Bulletin* launch on Friday 23rd November, we will have access to the beautiful Wren church, St Martin Within Ludgate in London, and will be putting on our biggest launch yet.

Finally, for those women members who are writers as well as readers of poetry, we have partnered with *Mslexia* and are running two major poetry competitions, the Women's Poetry Competition, judged by Carol Ann Duffy with a first prize of £2000 and the Women's Pamphlet Competition judged by Amy Wack, editor at Seren with a first prize of pamphlet publication by Seren. More details can be found on our website **www.poetrybooks.co.uk/competitions** or please do drop us a line or give us a call to hear more. The competitions are both open and the deadline for entry is 14th September.

We have a wonderful and challenging selection of poetry in this Autumn *Bulletin*, a thought-provoking mix of the political and the personal. We look forward to hearing your thoughts on the selections and hope you enjoy them as much as we have.

SOPHIE O'NEILL

PBS and Inpress Director

Image: Adine Sagalyn

# ELLEN HINSEY

Ellen Hinsey has published eight books of poetry, essays, dialogue and literary translation, including *Mastering the Past: Contemporary Central and Eastern Europe and the Rise of Illiberalism* (Telos Press, 2017). Her volumes of poetry include *Cities of Memory*, which received the Yale Series Award, *The White Fire of Time* and *Update on the Descent*, a National Poetry Series Finalist, which draws on her experience at the International Criminal Tribunal for the former Yugoslavia in The Hague. *Magnetic North: Conversations with Tomas Venclova / Ellen Hinsey* explores ethical experience under totalitarianism. A former faculty member of Skidmore College's Paris programme, she has been the recipient of numerous awards, including Lannan and Rona Jaffe Foundation fellowships. Hinsey's work has appeared in *The Poetry Review*, *The New York Times*, *The New Yorker*, *The Irish Times*, *The Paris Review* and *Poetry*. Selections have also been translated into French, Italian, German, Danish, Polish, Lithuanian, Serbian and Arabic. She lives in Paris and is the International Correspondent for *The New England Review*.

# THE ILLEGAL AGE

ARC | £10.99 | PBS PRICE £8.50

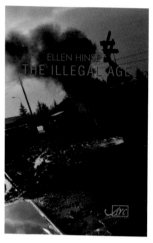

Ellen Hinsey's *The Illegal Age* follows on from her much-lauded poems and essays on human rights, conflict and authoritarianism. In three parts, or "investigation files", the book moves through and denatures several types of information-giving: reports, testimonies, handbooks, evidence. It is a complex structure, one that shifts in and out of the lyrical voice to relay two narratives: one that survives and resists violence and the other, a more powerful sanctioned history that attempts to silence it. The framework here is broadly the horrors of the second world war and consequences – from Poland to Stalin's Gulag camps to East Germany before reunification – but it frames an "illegal age" of totalitarianism and state violence that is intentionally familiar even today. Hinsey's writing is stunningly beautiful, and not without moments of dark humour, as she gathers her documents via quotations from some of the great witnesses of wartime and post-war Europe. Throughout the book the interwoven voices of poets Paul Celan, Ingeborg Bachmann, Czesław Miłosz and Wisława Szymborska echo, reminding readers that the crimes of the past could easily be repeated. Hinsey's poems recount the daily trials of hunger and loss alongside the interrogations of dictators whose moral certitude is its own madness. The pervasiveness of questioning, of the multitude of personal voices and so-called factual registers, unite in this book so convincingly that it is difficult to put it down. The book's epigraph, from Osip Mandelstam, who died under Stalin's hand, pleas "Forgive me for what I'm telling you". Hinsey's words are precisely this: tellings, new and old, that warn of the imperceptibility of power descending and taking everything away.

*Intimate Reflections*
At night in private, Power stares forlornly in the mirror,
secretly heartbroken that it isn't better loved.

*Nostalgia*
Power keeps a neat clipping file of its triumphs.

*Thoroughly Cliché, but Not Outmoded Strategy*
Power hopes that the People will eventually come to
love it, or if not, cease to exist.

*The Illegal Age* is an astonishing feat, an effortlessly humane book, one that must be read and balanced courageously against our own tumultuous times.

SANDEEP PARMAR

SELECTOR'S COMMENT

# ELLEN HINSEY

*When men are retaliating upon others, they are reckless of the future, and do not hesitate to annul those common laws of humanity to which every individual trusts for his own hope of deliverance should he ever be overtaken by calamity; they forget that in their own hour of need they will look for them in vain.*

*Reckless of the future* – we recognize ourselves in Thucydides' description of the decline of Athenian society. We witness the slow dissolution of bonds and laws that for a brief moment held things together. A shared future. *Each man was strong only in the conviction that nothing was secure; he must look to his own safety, and could not afford to trust others.* We search for the evidence behind us, the signs before us – how we arrived here. And what exactly is that: the shape of a shadowy future that approaches us on the horizon?

*The Illegal Age* was written over a period of eight years, crossing and re-crossing Western, and Eastern Europe. It is also a meditation on our past: the potential to set neighbor against neighbor. *Poetry as transcript. Poetry as evidence.* No longer Auden's "age of anxiety"; we now find we navigate in an open field without facts, with a diminishing sense of justice. *You too have felt it: the imperceptible shift in latitude.*

*Poetry as resistance.* A stranger, speaking aloud as he stared into a red sunset: "I wonder just what kind of future they are preparing for us." *Poetry as endurance.* Hannah Arendt's warning returns: "the first essential step on the road to total domination is to kill the juridical person in man." *Nothing happens quickly. There are indications, signposts, turns along the way.* And yet the movement, the risk is there: the advent of an Illegal Age.

## ELLEN RECOMMENDS

Hannah Arendt, *Men in Dark Times*; Ingeborg Bachmann, *In the Storm of Roses: Selected Poems*; Ana Blandiana, *The Sun Of Hereafter: Ebb of the Senses*; Václav Havel, *Open Letters*; Christine Lavant, *Shatter the Bell in My Ear*; Osip Mandelstam: *Poems* translated by James Greene; Czesław Miłosz, *The Captive Mind*; Miklós Radnóti, *Clouded Sky*; Georg Trakl, *Autumn Sonata*, translated by Daniel Simko.

I CHOICE

# XIX. EVIDENCE: THE ILLEGAL AGE (REPRISE)

You too have felt it: the imperceptible shift in latitude.

The way the air resistedly parts before the iron wedge
of storm.

Later, you will recall you once sensed it – in the instant of
darkness before daybreak, for which we have no name.

Do not think it has not been prepared; do not think
there are not those who are waiting.

Later, you will remember the air smelled of precision;
you will recollect how doubt wordlessly descended.

Was it in those final moments, when they were led down
to the water before the terrible act, that you first suspected?

You too will believe you were alone to perceive the
tenebrous advance heralded by manacles.

A way forward has been made for the hour without mercy.

Later, you will recall how each letter tightened in the
throat; the tongue stammering into silence.

Don't think your compliance is not being observed.

Later, you will realize that compromise is the wood
that burns most brightly in the hour before regret.

But by then, all the doors will have been marked in
yellow chalk.

Still, let us not pass each other this final time, without
recognition, without looking each other in the eye.

Remember: in the ink-light of testimony, a record may
still be kept.

Remember: in the ink-light of testimony, a record may still be kept.

# KIT FAN

Kit Fan was born in Hong Kong and moved to the UK aged 21. He studied at the Chinese University of Hong Kong before completing a doctoral thesis on Thom Gunn at the University of York. As well as being a published poet, he also writes fiction. In 2017 he was shortlisted for *The Guardian* 4th Estate BAME Short Story Prize for *Duty Free* and the *TLS* Mick Imlah Poetry Prize. In 2018 he won a Northern Writers' Award for *Diamond Hill*, a novel-in-progress portraying a deprived community in the last shanty town in Hong Kong during the 1980s. Kit's first book of poems *Paper Scissors Stone* won the inaugural HKU International Poetry Prize in 2011 and his translation of Classical Chinese poetry won one of *The Times* Stephen Spender Prizes in 2006. He reviews regularly for *The Poetry Review*. As his poetry moves between Hong Kong and European cultural histories, he also moves between poetry and narrative fiction. He lives in York and works in the Hull York Medical School.

# AS SLOW AS POSSIBLE

ARC | £9.99 | PBS PRICE £7.50

The title poem from Kit Fan's second collection *As Slow as Possible* corresponds with a piece of the same name by the avant-garde composer John Cage. The composition gives no indication of pace and in one recent interpretation it is skilfully being drawn out to last six hundred and thirty-nine years.

Having breathed six hundred and thirty-nine years, what remains of us will return to St. Burchardi in Halberstadt, the hometown of the first permanent pipe organ, in the six hundred and fortieth year of the third millennium, whether or not Earth has been forsaken...

What is technically possible and what is musically probable form a conundrum central to Fan's work. As the sandbags in St. Burchardi shift from organ pedal to pedal and notes elongate through the instrument's breath, time and mortality offer the major and minor notes:

the finished
sound, the tinnitus recalling absence.

Elsewhere, Fan's poems move melodically and rhythmically through personal loss, romantic and familial love, engaging aesthetically with the visible world and meditatively with the unseen. His writing is clear and effortless, languorous at times, reminiscent of the poet-traveller who seizes on an object and invests his own narrative force for civilisation in its frame. Here we find echoes of Elizabeth Bishop, Wallace Stevens, William Carlos Williams and perhaps a touch of James Merrill's elegant, flowing line.

At times political and ecological realities, the danger of death brushing close by, quickens the tempo: the Deepwater Horizon oil spill in the Gulf of Mexico, the 2014 Hong Kong protests (The Umbrella Movement) against Chinese erosions of democracy. The book's middle section, 'Genesis', collages Chinese creation myths and challenges the reader to rethink the accepted origins of everything including time, language, civilisation. Fan is a virtuoso of language and form, whose generous and sensitive ear make the reader pause and wait confidently for the next perfect note to strike.

# KIT FAN

As creatures of time, what are the differences between living at speed and living at a slow pace? One January, charged with the new year momentum but oppressed by the winter darkness of England (I had a sub-tropical birth and upbringing in Hong Kong), I discovered that John Cage's Organ²/ASLSP (As SLow aS Possible) has been playing in St. Burchardi in Halberstadt, Germany, since 2001 and is scheduled to play for six hundred and thirty-nine years, ending in 2640. Such slowness is to die for. Despite medical and technological investments in longevity and the afterlife, I won't, and don't want to, live to hear it end. It will have to finish without me and I'll have to finish without it being finished.

As some poems mushroom and evaporate, I find that those that stay with me speak to each other loosely and unconsciously about change and the unlikely bridges between far-flung places and times. They time-travel, shape-shift, and trans-migrate across geographies and time zones. They talk about death as much as about life (a bird, a painting, oil spills, trees, a cemetery, politics, lovemaking). Like me, they are creatures of time, speed and pace in their own right. I stole John Cage's title, knowing that I couldn't do it justice, but that justice is not the only thing I'm interested in.

The book is divided into three parts, pivoting around a central sequence 'Genesis', which re-tells Chinese creation myths in the language of the Authorised Version. Part I is a book of changes, reporting from time-and-space travels. It ends with a more grounded calendrical sequence 'Twelve Months', a kind of poetic house-keeping. It's a privilege to play with the gods, but Earth is definitely more fun and dazzling. As William Blake said, "Eternity is in Love with the Productions of Time."

## KIT RECOMMENDS

Jenny Xie's *Eye Level* is a mesmerising debut. I was carried away by what Robin Robertson did to – and with – poetry, fiction and cinema in *The Long Take*. I would like to have been Basho's travel companion when he wrote *The Records of a Weather-Exposed Skeleton*. I am excited to read Emily Wilson's new translation of *The Odyssey* over the summer. I love listening to Alice Oswald's *Dart* on the plane. My week lacks savour without a dose of Emily Dickinson.

and my mind hiding in the thicket of a burning tree

Image: Ffiona Lewis

# THE NIGHT SWITCH

This is a sanctuary, you say, turning a page,
dotting the marginalia while my pixelated eyes
scan the news, weather, dust in Syria, soiling
the bed with white light pulsating through the night.
There's not enough darkness in the mind.
In the mind my mother's bleached, fluorescent hands
counting money, in the background the radio
humming the news, weather, Vietnamese refugees,
and me, lonely as a bird, swallowing the cry
of the jingling coins. She still does it every night,
counting, then, switching off the light in the corridor,
her silhouette glowing in the traffic as if on fire
and my mind hiding in the thicket of a burning tree.

# ANDREW McMILLAN

Andrew McMillan's debut collection *physical* was the first ever poetry collection to win *The Guardian* First Book Award. The collection also won the Fenton Aldeburgh First Collection Prize, a Somerset Maugham Award, an Eric Gregory Award and a Northern Writers' Award. It was shortlisted for the Dylan Thomas Prize, the Costa Poetry Award, *The Sunday Times* Young Writer of the Year 2016, the Forward Prize for Best First Collection, the Roehampton Poetry Prize and the Polari First Book Prize. It was a Poetry Book Society Recommendation for Autumn 2015. *physical* has been translated into Norwegian (Aschehoug, 2017) and a bilingual French edition, *Le Corps Des Hommes* (Grasset, 2018). He is senior lecturer at the Manchester Writing School at MMU and lives in Manchester.

# PLAYTIME

ANDREW
McMILLAN

playtime

CAPE POETRY

CAPE | £10.00 | PBS PRICE £7.50

Byron accused Keats of "frigging his imagination"; Thom Gunn riffed mischievously on Wordsworth's definition of poetry, suggesting that verses claiming to be "spontaneous overflows of powerful feeling" amount, finally, to "wet dreams, wet dreams, in libraries congealing". Masturbation isn't sex: it's solipsistic, it doesn't touch another person (except mentally); but Andrew McMillan writes so sensitively about it. He considers – the privilege, as well as the burden, of one type of gay poet? – vulnerabilities we don't usually talk about, taking the private feelings of men seriously. A "posh wank", if you didn't know, involves a condom:

> ...then afterwards
> something like peeling back a stocking
> a possible life seeping out the end
> you didn't know to knot before binning
> the tiny deaths you would come to know
> the smell of    and their ghoststains on the sheets

Orgasm has been compared to "la petite mort" – a little death – so McMillan is talking about future encounters, with other men, in a "possible life", as well as the tiny deaths of umpteen sperm: the suggestion is that, even when another person touches him, the speaker remains alone. The poem isn't a one-off: it rewards re-reading. McMillan admires Gunn, is influenced by him, and he has also written smartly, in *Poetry Review*, about the doubts and second-thoughts which Tom Paulin adds to his verse by means of dashes. This poet's equivalent is the white space, which appears in his lines to mark either a moment of emphasis or a plunge in a new direction, giving his verse a tactile spontaneity:

> without a word from you I  know to take my tongue
>
> and run it the length of your back  base  of  spine
> to ears   where the teeth will let themselves be heard
>
> its not a straight line that does it   but rather
> random lappings  like  spots of rain before a storm

# ANDREW McMILLAN

When I was in Year 8 of secondary school, our teacher wheeled in an old TV with a VCR attached; this was sex education and we were going to watch an informative video. The only bit of it I remember at all is an earnest voice-over saying: "when a man becomes sexually aroused, he may become flustered and want to take his jumper off". That's all; and that's what passed for sex education at the turn of the new millennium in my village just outside Barnsley.

More and more I've been thinking about how it is that we grow into our sexual selves; how we discover things about our own bodies, how we then bring our bodies into conversation and contact with other peoples'. The first half of this collection inhabits childhood and early adolescence, and almost by necessity these are intensely awkward poems, to write if not to read, about "first times", about sexting and sex, about coming out, about growing into the embarrassment and clumsiness of our own teenage bodies; I'm pushing myself as much as possible to write into a place of extreme discomfort. If *physical* was a book about me (or people like me) in my early twenties, a lot of these poems are going back in time, thinking about how it was I became the person I was in that first book.

Beyond that, I'm interested in pursuing the things I always have been, mainly that sweaty, difficult, fascinating place where sex, sexuality, masculinity and class all rub up against each other. The people who didn't like my first book (you know who you are!) will definitely not like this one; but to them I say: Relax, pour yourself a drink, take off your jumper.

## ANDREW RECOMMENDS

In an age that seems to celebrate and bemoan, in equal measure, glibness, transience and brevity, I'm becoming more and more interested in the resurgence of the long poem, of the book as whole object rather than accumulation of occasional poems. Hannah Sullivan's *Three Poems*, Layli Long Soldier's *Whereas* and Robin Robertson's *The Long Take* are all great recent examples. For my own book, the bravery and craft of Sam Willetts is always inspiring and Mark Doty and Sharon Olds are the poets I hold closest to my heart as I write.

RECOMMENDATION

they sit arguing the terms of how
their bodies will exist together
how they will survive the knowing of each other

# WHAT 1.6% OF YOUNG MEN KNOW

to get the body of their favourite sports star
they must starve themselves      that the muscles
are there already    if they could only
get at them       that the thing to do is eat less
and replace meals with water   so that they bloat
and then feel their insides flushing out

that the stomach will expand and shrink back
like a gas holder in a former
industrial town       that once the body
has burned off all its fat    it will start on muscle
that more exercise just gives more energy
for the body to eat itself alive

that they can forget what it's like to stand
without feeling dizzy    that their eyesight
can fail      that their salad can be carried
in smaller and smaller tupperware boxes
that the doctor will be forced
to ban the gym   will deliver his prognosis

that they will end up in the carpark of the doctors
with their mum saying *imagine  a child of mine  malnourished*

Image: Naomi Woddis

# FIONA MOORE

Fiona Moore lives in Greenwich. She has an MBA in organisational culture and a degree in Classics. In 2004 she left her Foreign Office career to write and worked part-time for Excellent Development, the sand dam charity. She helped edit *The Rialto* for several years and is co-editing an issue of *Magma* on climate change for late 2018. She swims, walks (ideally up a hill), reviews poetry and blogs occasionally at displacement-poetry.blogspot. com. Her first pamphlet, *The Only Reason for Time*, was a *Guardian* Poetry Book of the Year and her second, *Night Letter*, was shortlisted for the Michael Marks Awards.

RECOMMENDATION

# THE DISTAL POINT

HAPPENSTANCE | £10.00 | PBS PRICE £7.50

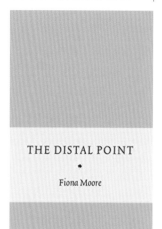

THE DISTAL POINT

•

Fiona Moore

In this collection, the poet's fine ear often performs a kind of grief-work. 'Overwinter' begins:

> This is midwinter's longest day
> that absorbs its own silence of waiting.

Moore isn't embarrassed to be a poet: she refines her language, tinting its twists and turns, confident it will shine with meaning. The longest day of winter waits on spring, but this is also a description of the speaker's unexpressed feelings:

> Nothing moves through the air
> and gravity seems a miracle, the earth's grip
> made of so much more than frost.

Again, there is the plain idea (no clouds, no rain, no snow) and then a creative reckoning with feelings elusive of summary – the alliteration is quietly intense –

> Instead the ground-mist floats the trees
> whose outlines are all gesture,
> each miming the wait differently.

A poem can be visual but can never be a painting: the uncertainties of language see to that (consider what "instead" is doing here); and in these lines, which remind me of Elizabeth Bishop's 'Questions of Travel', we each discover a different picture.

> Nothing will happen for a while, nothing—
> and I need such certainty: to become
> embedded deep within this season
> when dark overplaits the day's pale strand.

"Nothing" ripens: so much is silently changing, beneath the snow and within the person speaking to us. The line-break highlights the phrase "to become"– she, too, will flower like spring – but the following line suggests, instead, a withdrawal, like a bear's period of hibernation. This captures a moment of emotional ambivalence: the assonance linking "overplaits" and "pale strand" provides – again – far more than a nicely-turned phrase.

> Change may come while nothing seems to change.
> I know it will take a long time.

The bare facts again – "long" returns us to the start – but we, like its speaker, come out of the poem stronger than we went in. "While", "seems", "nothing": the most basic-seeming words have produced a small miracle.

| SELECTOR'S COMMENT VIDYAN RAVINTHIRAN

# FIONA MOORE

"Contemporary poets do not aspire to 'greatness'; the role they are meant to fulfil is the role of the earthworm. The soil of the earthworm is language." I wish I'd written that but it was the Polish poet Wojciech Bonowicz.

Poems tend to fall short of the writer's hopes: fail again, fail better. Where does that leave a book containing fifty five of them, fifty five attempts to aerate and redistribute language? Anyway, the poems determined the book rather than the other way round. The collection-making process was instinctive, like collaging scraps of writing into a poem: rearranging, discarding and adding until the result felt OK. Then it was possible to apply structure and logic – and it's only in these terms that I can talk about *The Distal Point*.

The book's first part, 'Overwinter', is a response to my partner's early death. 'Exclave', the mostly political middle section, includes poems set in the dark days of Eastern Europe where "the walls of the museum are papered with lies". I lived there in the mid-1980s. The third, called 'The Rose, the Stars' (which I nearly chose as the title because no-one would dare use anything so poetic), addresses eternal themes of love, death, public transport, the non-linearity of time, a cardboard box, outer space and woodpeckers: "Red nape and undertail: for desire, for hope / against the dust and woodworm in its echo".

The distal point itself is a geological term found in a hut on Orford Ness off the Suffolk coast; here it refers to a shingle spit's far end, "the point of greatest change". I hope my endless Anthropocene-age anxiety about climate change and species loss infuses at least some of the poems.

Do earthworms eat poets? The world's largest search engine won't give me a straight answer.

## FIONA RECOMMENDS

*The Last Two Seconds*, Mary Jo Bang (Graywolf); *Swims*, Elizabeth Jane Burnett (Penned in the Margins); *Pool Epitaphs and Other Love Letters*, Ágnes Lehóczky (Boiler House Press); *Basic Nest Architecture*, Polly Atkin (Seren); *Bad Kid Catullus*, edited by Kirsten Irving & Jon Stone (Sidekick). Exciting reading among 2018's many first collections; one deserving more attention is *Gall* by Matt Howard (Rialto). Looking forward to: Kathryn Maris' latest; first collections from Zaffar Kunial, Layli Long Soldier and Jay Bernard (2019).

RECOMMENDATION

We stand at the point of greatest change—
the distal point, a shingle spit

# THE SHIRT

I didn't find it for months, your shirt
bundled into a corner in the airing cupboard.
I shook it out. It had been cut
with long cuts all the way up the sleeves
and up the front, so it looked like a plan
of something about to be put together.
They must have had to work so fast to
save you there was no time to unbutton it.
An office shirt, because that's where
it happened. The thin stripes slashed through—
terrifying, unprecedented— a reminder
of everything I wanted to forget.
I'd washed it afterwards, not knowing what to do
with it, or that in three weeks the same thing
would happen to another shirt, a favourite,
dull cotton whose thick weave made it look
as if all the pink shell-grains of sand
had come together on one beach,
a shirt for a gentle hug; and from then on
nothing happened that we would forget.

# KATE POTTS

Kate Potts' debut pamphlet *Whichever Music* (tall-lighthouse, 2008) was a Poetry Book Society Pamphlet Choice and was shortlisted for a Michael Marks Award. Her first full-length collection was *Pure Hustle* (Bloodaxe Books, 2011). Kate teaches poetry and creative writing for the University of Oxford, Middlesex University and The Poetry School, freelances as a mentor and editor, and works part-time for an independent publisher. She has been awarded two Arts Council England grants and a Hawthornden Fellowship. Her second collection *Feral* sets out to explore and trouble the boundary between "animal" and "human".

# FERAL

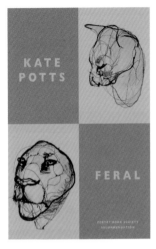

BLOODAXE | £9.95 | PBS PRICE £7.47

As the title suggests, Kate Potts is interested in animals – their rights, their forms of consciousness – and also in overturning the sort of humanism which sees us as separate to them, deified by our intelligence. On the contrary, what we are, first and foremost, is our bodies, and in 'Footnotes to a Long-Distance Telephone Call' – they really are footnotes! – she positions her voice as proceeding directly from her flesh: "I'm calling from the space we'll call 'my body': 5'9 and 144lb, beige skin, twenty-five teeth, short-sight in one eye (heritage: Nottinghamshire, Leicestershire, Staffordshire, Norfolk, Taff Valley; shopkeeper, farm-hand, forester, gardener, prison officer, market trader, typist, scullery maid, cook, wife, teacher, lecturer, Londoner)." She also says – acknowledging the politics of identity we must all wade through then leap free of – "I'm calling from nowhere but nowhere but the blank page: horizon, all the wild blue distance." This unbridled creativity issues in segmented prose, mutinously bedraggled long lines, and – when she does hone more overtly – a compression recalling Keats' determination to "load every rift with ore":

> Beyond your window trees gripe, winded, and the air glowers gunmetal,
> while sparrows fret and the sky creaks shut its velvet hinge, I spin your lullaby.

Language jolts towards touch (the vowels, the consonants, in your mouth), insisting on a life of sensations as well as thoughts. On every page of this determinedly hybrid, multi-part, conceptual book appear such flares of momentary brilliance which transmit, as acutely as possible, a vitality which is only hers to hold for a moment.

This deepest layer might, we imagine, be Proterezoic: a stratum of bacteria conserved in garden clay and builder's slate; see – the imprint of a child's tooth suspended in resin; here a fossilised pang of Vaporub, bath suds, the boozy wallop of milk.

I was disappointed, recently, to read – is it real news, or fake? – of Donald Trump framing on his wall an aphorism of William Blake's, which I previously admired: "the road of excess leads to the palace of wisdom". Really, it belongs on the back of this compelling second collection.

| SELECTOR'S COMMENT

VIDYAN RAVINTHIRAN

# KATE POTTS

*Feral* took shape over a period of seven years. After *Pure Hustle* I worked hard to explore and develop my voice, both on the page and in performance. I've often been wary of "the personal". In recent years I've been thinking about how female writers – Anne Carson, Emily Berry and Solmaz Sharif for example – navigate the "lyric I". I'm increasingly aware of just how intensely political "the personal" can be. In *Feral* I wanted to work shamelessly with parts of my experience that have tended to feel excluded, invisible, or problematic in everyday conversation. I'm interested in the ways in which the idea of "the animal" is used to maintain and police borders and power structures, particularly in terms of class, race, and gender. I also wanted to explore the idea of "feral" as outside, or in the borderlands of, language and the human. John Berger's *Why Look at Animals?* and Joanna Bourke's essay *Are Women Animals?* were both useful reference points.

In my teaching I'm intrigued by the way students tend to think of "nature" as separate and external to them. I've been thinking and writing, inevitably, about humans' dysfunctional relationship with the environment, and with the rest of the species on the planet. The animals in *Feral* began insistently sneaking their way into the book through the dictionary definition poems, in which abstract definition gives way to language that's specific, contextual, and often narrative. While working on the poems that make up *Feral* I was also writing *The Blown Definitions*, a radio play for multiple voices. The extracts of *The Blown Definitions* I've included in the book, with their discussion of home, language, and belonging, seem like necessary counterpoint and context.

## KATE RECOMMENDS

Svetlana Alexievich, *Chernobyl Prayer* (Penguin); John Berger and Sean Mohr, *A Seventh Man* (Verso); Jane Commane, *Assembly Lines* (Bloodaxe); Kayo Chingonyi, *Kumukanda* (Chatto); Stuart Cooke (ed.), George Dyungayan's *Bulu Line: A West Kimberley Song Cycle* (Puncher & Wattmann); Emily Dickinson, *Letters* (Everyman); Marie Howe, *What the Living Do* (Norton); Amy Key, *Isn't Forever* (Bloodaxe); Layli Long Soldier, *Whereas* (Graywolf Press); Cathy Park Hong, *Dance Dance Revolution* (Norton); Abigail Parry, *Jinx* (Bloodaxe); Solmaz Sharif, *Look* (Graywolf Press).

| RECOMMENDATION

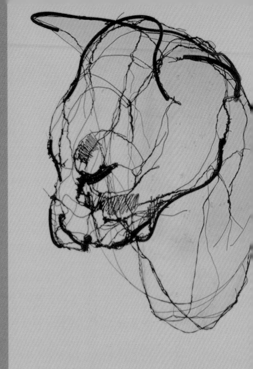

...the blank page: horizon, all the wild blue distance

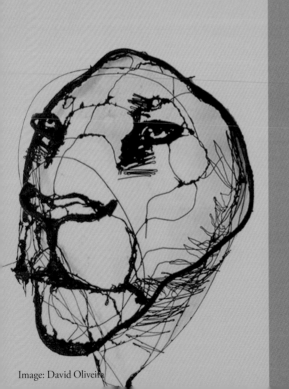

Image: David Oliveira

# ANIMAL SONG (I)

Adults had sparse hair on their bodies,
except for thick shocks at the scalp,
        underarm, and pubic bone.

They measured, on average, 1.65 metres
tall. They walked steady on their
        hind legs, like startled bears.

They spent their lives on land,
   worked out their days to the sea's
        slackening beat.

They were cossetted by stores
     of insulating body fat and by
scale-like or feather-like armour.

They hunted, insatiate, in packs.
   They huddled in groups, or hived
in pods of silicon, lime, and stone.

At night they covered their eyes to plumb
their own neural playback, experiment
     with impulse and response,
observe the shadow-play
        of electrical storms.

At night they met to breed, dived –
subaqueous – inside each other's skins;
they choreographed aerobic dances.

Fossil remains of humanoid
    bodies discovered in East Africa
are 350,000 years old.

They apportioned *worth* – the value of
time, matter, or bodies – in terms
    of potential exchange.

They killed with an iron tool,
    a blow to the back of the head,
a mechanised procession/ poison,
    detonation, a slow
        privation.

Image: Alice-Andrea Ewing

# LOLA RIDGE

Born in Ireland, raised in New Zealand and reaching artistic maturity in New York, Lola Ridge was transnational long before the termed gained currency. She established herself as one of the most notable American poets of her time with the publication of *The Ghetto* in 1918 and continued to write socially and spiritually conscious poetry up until her death in 1941.

Daniel Tobin is the author of eight books of poems and editor of *The Book of Irish American Poetry from the Eighteenth Century to the Present* and *Light in the Hand: Early Selected Poems of Lola Ridge*. He has received a Robert Frost Fellowship as well as fellowships from the Nationa Endowment for the Arts and the John Simon Guggenheim Foundation. Tobin teaches at Emerson College, Boston.

SPECIAL COMMENDATION

# TO THE MANY: COLLECTED EARLY WORKS
## EDITED BY DANIEL TOBIN

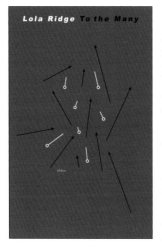

LITTLE ISLAND PRESS | £14 | PBS PRICE £10.50

It is high time that the Irish-born American poet Lola Ridge was read more widely, especially given the political domain of her writing. Ridge's poetry, introduced here by scholar Daniel Tobin, spans early twentieth-century battlegrounds over the rights of women, the poor and the worker. This edition is compiled from Ridge's early books *The Ghetto and Other Poems* (1918), *Sun-Up and Other Poems* (1920), *Red Flag* (1927), as well as poems from her first, more formal, book *Verses* (1905). Ridge's 1919 essay *Woman and the Creative Will* appears here, too, which meditates on the absence of canonical female writers and the androgyny of the artist's mind a near decade before Virginia Woolf's famous lecture-turned-book *A Room of One's Own* broke similar ground. A feminist anarchist critical of America's social divisions and the growing power of capitalism, Ridge constructs moral empathy in her depictions of the oppressed.

> Here ye, Dictators – late Lords of the Iron,
> Shut in your council rooms, palsied, depowered –
> The blooded, implacable Word?
> Not whispered in cloture, one to the other,
> (Brother in fear of the fear of his brother ...)
> But chanted and thundered
> On the brazen, articulate tongues of the Iron
> Babbling in flame ...

It is uncanny reading 'The Ghetto', a long poem that opens this volume. In Ridge's poetry we find accounts of the multicultural crucible of America's cities alongside prejudice and intolerance, most controversially in 'Lullaby', an incident of terrible racial violence from the East St. Louis riots. Responding to the urban miseries and social tensions across her adopted country, but most especially Manhattan's Lower East Side, Ridge could just as easily be speaking to the wider political turmoil of twenty-first-century America. She is a poet who finds a vital poetic language for human need, suffering and injustice – and one that must continue to be heard.

# WIND RISING IN THE ALLEYS

Wind rising in the alleys
My spirit lifts in yours like a banner
    streaming free of hot walls.
You are full of unspent dreams …
Your laden with beginnings …
There is hope in you … not sweet …
        acrid as blood in the mouth.
Come into my tossing dust
Scattering the peace of old deaths,
Wind rising in the alleys,
Carrying stuff of flame.

# SEXTUS
# PROPERTIUS

*Carcanet*
*Classics*

*edited & translated by*
Patrick Worsnip

*Poems*

✓

# SEXTUS PROPERTIUS

Sextus Propertius, the late Augustan poet, is best known today from Pound's famous 'Homage', less translation than brilliant experiment. Patrick Worsnip's new versions rise out of the Latin and brilliantly recreate the poet's voice, his life and loves (Cynthia in particular), when Rome was in full late flower. He was an elegist and a celebrator whose music rises again in these new versions.

Patrick Worsnip read Classics and Modern Languages at Merton College, Oxford, and worked for more than forty years as a correspondent and editor for Reuters news agency in more than eighty countries, specialising in diplomatic affairs. Since retiring in 2012, he has devoted himself to translation from Italian and Latin and to magazine articles on Italian poetry. He divides his time between Cambridge and Umbria, Italy.

# SEXTUS PROPERTIUS
## TRANSLATED BY PATRICK WORSNIP

CARCANET | £12.99 | PBS PRICE £9.75

There are so many different kinds of translation to choose from this time that any choice would be difficult. How do you balance a contemporary poet, newly translated into English, with a major text like Hafez, beautifully translated by Mario Petrucci, *Beowulf*, translated by Chris McCully, or Patrick Worsnip's *Sextus Propertius*? Maybe, this time, the choice had to come from those three, though I was also much tempted by Kristín Ómarsdóttir's selected poems, *Waitress in Fall* translated from the Icelandic by Vala Thorodds.

It was the sheer ambition of Sextus Propertius that caught my eye. Propertius was an elegiac poet of Ancient Rome, probably best known to us through Ezra Pound's 'Homage to Sextus Propertius'. Previous, closer translations of Propertius by Pound do exist but this new one, the translator of which rejects the term elegy and prefers to talk of "personal poem", seems to me the best of the popular editions. Propertius writes love poetry, much as Catullus did, in Propertius's case to a woman called Cynthia, and Worsnip catches the ardour and oddly modern gabbiness of its texture.

> What's the sense, darling, going out
> in a fancy coiffure, swinging the sheer pleats
> of an outfit from Kos, plastering your hair
> with oriental "product"? Imported finery
> makes *you* the product.
> - Book I.2

"Coiffure", "outfit", and "product" lodge the tone in a demotic that is not too self-conscious and yet is distinctly of "now".

> Everything you see here, friend, where the megacity of Rome
> now stands was hills and grass till Trojan Aeneas settled,
> - Book IV. 1

There it is "megacity" that kicks us into the present. The translation is play as well as passion and, despite the scholarship of the introduction and the generous notes at the end, the book is characterised by spirit, desire and a briskness of touch that makes the reading of these "personal poems" a valuable pleasure.

GEORGE SZIRTES

SELECTOR'S COMMENT

# BOOK 1.1

Cynthia was first, her eyes
made me her abject prisoner-of-war.
I had till then been untouched by Amor,
who now pulled down the vanity of my glance,
trampled my head with his feet.
That villain taught me to despise
respectable girls and lead an aimless life.
It's a year now this lunacy won't leave me,
the whole pantheon ranged against me.

Tullus, you've read that Milanion shirked nothing
to break down the contempt of Atalanta.
He roamed demented through Arcadian wilds,
killed beasts, was wounded by the centaur's club,
made the rocks echo with his moans …
And so tamed the girl sprinter,
such is the power of word and deed in love.

My slow-witted passion can think up no such tricks,
the map from the past is forgotten.
But you who claim you can bring down the moon
and appease spirits with magic fires,
now's your chance! Change the mind of my beloved,
let her pallor exceed mine!
Then I'll believe you can summon
stars and ghosts with your witches' songs.

Image: Jill Furmanovsky

# SELIMA HILL

Selima Hill's poetry has won the Cholmondeley, Whitbread and Michael Marks Awards. She was shortlisted for the Forward, T.S. Eliot, Costa and Roehampton Poetry Prizes. Her most recent collections include *People Who Like Meatballs* (Bloodaxe, 2012), shortlisted for both the Forward Poetry Prize and the Costa Poetry Award; *Jutland* (2015), a Poetry Book Society Special Commendation which was shortlisted for the 2015 T.S. Eliot Prize and the Roehampton Poetry Prize; *The Magnitude of My Sublime Existence* (2016), shortlisted for the Roehampton Poetry Prize 2017; and *Splash Like Jesus* (2017).

# FISHTANK

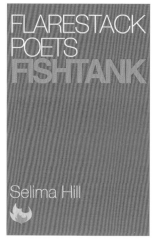

FLARESTACK POETS | £6.00

A reader may enter a Selima Hill text in the same way that a frog enters a pot of cold water. The environment is new but the reader is still happily froggy. By imperceptible degrees, however, the elements begin to jostle; by a miracle of stealth, the reader's mind is slowly transformed into a heavenly hot delicacy.

I remember exactly where I was when I first read *A Little Book of Meat*, her 1993 Bloodaxe collection: sitting at a summer table outside Òran Mór at the top of Byres Road in Glasgow. It was one of those very rare things in a poetry collection – a gripping page-turner. I was utterly hooked. This pamphlet from Flarestack Poets is no less memorable, a testament to Hill's remarkable longevity at this level of creative ingenuity.

In *Fishtank*, the narrator is concerned with telling us about her older brother, primarily from a child's-eye view. This allows for a series of puzzlements about masculinity, relationships and societal norms, while newly-minted certainties arise from existential ambiguities. This is the poem 'My Brother's Shoes' in its entirety:

> Men who wear suede shoes are all *cads*
> so when my brother creeps into the kitchen
>
> wearing what appear to be suede shoes
> I naturally conclude he's not my brother.

Hill manages to make the narrator-brother relationship extraordinarily tender and at the same time theoretical – the narrator attempts to construct a brother-image by gathering small clues, turning evidence, keeping the red herrings just in case. She also acknowledges, not without anxiety, the flux and mutability inherent in the human condition:

> I *do not like it* when he plays the flute
> because he is transformed: he leaves behind
>
> the man he was and becomes a man
> who seems to want to break his own heart.
>
> – 'My Brother's Flute'

# MY BROTHER IN TENNIS SHORTS

He's found a ball and some enormous shorts
and yellow sandshoes tied with yellow string.

His hair is thick and rigid like a privet hedge.
His unforced errors make my heart sink.

# MY BROTHER'S SPECTACLES

On summer afternoons he can be found
reading from an ancient book – or staring at it,

like a large and flightless bird in spectacles
that's spent a million years in captivity.

# MY BROTHER'S SHOULDERS

I sit here for a very long time.
Suddenly my brother reappears,

puts me on his shoulders and strides off.
I'm not as happy as I ought to be

because he keeps on begging me (with threats)
*not to keep on stroking his eyelids.*

SELIMA HILL

45

# US
## ZAFFAR KUNIAL

FABER | £10.99 | PBS PRICE £8.25

Zaffar Kunial's *Us* works as a pensive and rich meditation on belonging, migration, identity and language. Each poem offers keen and original insight into the complex duality of personhood when investigated through the optics of race, religion, colonialism and grief.

The opening poem 'Fielder' sits as a soft and striking piece in its ability to still time and distance. The moment in the poem where the speaker says, "And when I reflect, here, from this undiscovered city, / well north of those boyish ambitions – for the county, / maybe later, the country – I know something of that minute / holds something of me, there, beyond the boundary, in that edgeland of central England", acts as a precursor for what's to follow – a reoccurring sensibility which manoeuvres and reforms as the collection progresses.

Like much of Kunial's poetry, one often finds themselves to be drawn into an unembellished yet magical world by way of a language both considered and private. In the poem 'W\*ind' the opening stanza declares: "When I arrived / I didn't know / the word / for what I was." Reminiscent of Layli Long Soldier's collection *Whereas*, a masterful book which sets out to subvert, reclaim and reorganise standardised forms of writing, many of the speakers we meet throughout Kunial's poems seem to possess a similar desire – to re-establish some sense of place in a home away from home using a broken and foreign syntax.

'Prayer', a Highly Commended poem in the 2017 Forward Prize, typifies Kunial's skill not only as a raconteur but as a poet who's able to move seamlessly between the agony of losing a parent and the reverence of birthing a child, while suspending both events on the idea of a prayer: "I'd keep in thought my mum on a Hereford hospital bed / and say what prayer couldn't end. I'd say I made an animal noise / hurled language's hurt // at midday, when word had come."

*Us* is a masterful and painstaking look at the complexities of identity which transcend the glib and theoretical, shifting daringly between past and present.

WILD CARD CHOICE

ANTHONY ANAXAGOROU

# ANTHONY ANAXAGOROU

ANTHONY ANAXAGOROU has published nine volumes of poetry, a spoken-word EP and a collection of short stories. His work has appeared on BBC Newsnight, Radio 4, ITV and Sky Arts as well as being published in *The Feminist Review*, Amnesty International's *Words That Burn* and John Berger's anthology *The Long White Thread of Words*. He was commissioned by the Labour Party during the 2017 general election to write their campaign poem. In 2015 he won the Groucho Maverick Award and in 2016 he was shortlisted for the Hospital Club's H-100 award for influential people. In 2012 he founded Out-Spoken, London's premier poetry and music night, and Out-Spoken Press, an independent publisher which challenges the lack of diversity in British publishing.

WILD CARD SELECTOR

# ZAFFAR KUNIAL

Why *Us*? The word "us" to me looks like an extract from the middle of other words. Ho*us*e. Conf*us*ed.

The poem called 'Us' partly began as I stared absent-mindedly at a book cover – with a picture of Marilyn Monroe, reading Joyce – *Ulysses and Us*. I was struck by how Ulysses was contained, compressed between the letters of "Us" and thought of how Odysseus also has that word at the end, and of how we enclose our journeys and stories, and how they hold us, like a book.

Because my book is called *Us* I wanted the poems to feel both various but also interconnected – but naturally so, and I took my time to let this happen. I wanted the book to offer that kind of satisfaction a novel gives when its connections become a kind of gravity. The first books I read were story books, and *Us* tells a kind of story. Mine and not mine at once, one signed uncertainly with "yours". The word "story" appears nine times in the book (eleven if you include *kahani* which means the same) and the word "yours" appears eight times (ten if you include *tuwarda* and *tusaanda*). Some words and names are almost like characters in a story, characters with histories that interlink, even down to the letter.

And letters in both senses. The last poem 'Ys' is partly about an airmail letter my mother sent to my father in Kashmir, and about a laburnum tree I knew before I could read. Perhaps "Us" could also be seen as the plural of "u".

In the comments section, under her *Guardian* Poem of the Week article about *Us*, Carol Rumens wrote: "He picks up certain words and wave-patterns across poems, too... 'Stamping Grounds' is the title of two poems, an 'earlier' and a 'later', each with its post office, and English grandfather, Stan, 'whose name in my father's language means land'... Only connect. The connections themselves connect, and the reader become a kind of reader-bee, a happy messenger going to and fro, brushed with pollen."

In *The Poetry Review* a couple of years ago I wrote about my poetic "omphalos" which I struggled to put into words, but this was the coda to it: "The god of the sky in Greek lore, Zeus, once sent his own kind of airmail from the ends of the earth – two eagles, released simultaneously – one from the east, and one from the west. They flew towards each other, over the seas and lands in between till they met at the centre of the earth. Uncertain as I often am, I'm not sure I have anything as sturdy or unshifting as a poetic earth-centre, but if I did, on a good day, it might be my tree. That stubborn, yellow-flowering, time-telling laburnum, despite its tiny particles that tightened my breath. Or maybe – to be more particular – that dusty hiding place, up there, unshiftably sturdy in the crook of the trunk's Y."

# BOOK REVIEWS

## FONDUE: A.K. BLAKEMORE

Blakemore constructs a curious series of impressions, brought to life in carefully selected language, the rhythmic and phonetic quality of which is crisply calculated. Sexual expression, musings upon self, the other and abstract observation become entangled in a complex but vivid sequence. At one point the poet is cast as "a child harpist // and everyone else and their sufferings // are strings". Yet Blakemore's performative personhood, whether occupying the poetic voice or being viewed by it, is certainly not childlike, having a mature but lively self-assurance.

OFFORD ROAD BOOKS | £10.00 | PBS PRICE £7.50

## THE HOTEL EDEN: BEVERLEY BIE BRAHIC

The poems in this collection are energised by themes of temporal and spatial progression. Seasons move on with a dream-like quality, the warm, hazy summer poems of the first part slipping into the cooler tones of autumn and winter as the poetic voice moves from place to place. Plants grow, bees buzz and the rural, provincial and domestic become transcendent. An exquisitely poetic sequence.

CARCANET | £9.99 | PBS PRICE £7.50

## BRAGR: ROSS COGAN

*Bragr* starts with a retelling of the Norse creation story and then slowly slides from the epic to the personal. However, myth still informs its symbols and preoccupations. The central part of this bold and striking collection is a "bestiary", the lives and deaths of animals passing before the poet's eyes. This being and undoing is mirrored in the final section 'Ragnarok', the end of the world, where myth grips the reins once more and sends the reader plunging into a lyrical abyss.

SEREN BOOKS | £9.99 | PBS PRICE £7.50

Fred D'Aguiar's translations form radical *re*memberings of a range of characters from the ancient to the present, Homer to Derek Walcott. Each is seen through the patois prism of a Guyanese poet translated to America. Western and Eastern philosophies converge – hellenists versus hedonists – with odes to Africa and the pervasive shadow of slavery. These re-imaginings speak through cultural difference, familiarity and otherness, to transform elegy into celebration.

CARCANET | £12.99 | PBS PRICE £9.75

———— BELOVED: 81 POEMS FROM HAFEZ ————
TRANSLATED BY MARIO PETRUCCI

Mario Petrucci renders the 14th century Persian poet Hafez into English with delicacy and musicality. These vital versions capture the rich multiplicity of Hafez' sensual and spiritual intensity. His "love-luminous" ghazals are intoxicated with the beauty of "the full white moon", roses and nightingales and lit by life-affirming mantras: "Reader: don't give in to dust. Each cloud must lift."

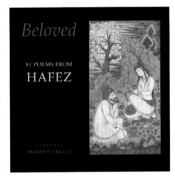

BLOODAXE | £12.00 | PBS PRICE £9.00

———— ONE LARK, ONE HORSE: MICHAEL HOFMANN ————

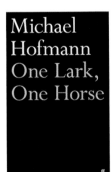

Hofmann's love of vocabulary and wordplay shine through in this collection, which takes its title from a joke attributed to Primo Levi about paté. Prolific, irrepressible verse bursts from these pages. The occasional short poem serves almost as a pause for breath. This is Hofmann's first new poetry collection since 1999 and is a wonderful return to the form, the poet's unique perspective drawing in a panoply of subjects functioning as a kind of sublime biography.

FABER | £14.99 (HB) | PBS PRICE £11.25

BOOK REVIEWS |

## GAIA HOLMES: WHERE THE ROAD RUNS OUT

Holmes chronicles the stages of grief – the awareness of approaching death, the loss and the recovery – with searing lyricism. This emotional journey, with all of its turns, is met with adroit and luminous verse. Insightful and often witty, Holmes faces the trials of life not only with her deft elegiac touch but with reserves of humour.

COMMA PRESS | £9.99 | PBS PRICE £7.50

## CLIVE JAMES: THE RIVER IN THE SKY

James writes: "it is my turn looming / To plot an exit from the world". And so this single, long-form poem is preoccupied with memory, life and mortality – a poignant but often witty memoir flitting back and forth from subject to subject in measured, economical but elegant language. *The River in the Sky* is a modern epic, referencing the grand sweep of cultural and literary history, from the ancient past through to the clatter of the twentieth century and beyond.

PICADOR | £14.99 | PBS PRICE £11.25

## WRETCHED STRANGERS: EDITED BY ÁGNES LEHÓCZKY & JT WELSCH

Coinciding with the second anniversary of Brexit, this anthology celebrates the wide range of migrant writers who contribute to British poetry culture and counters the recent rise in nationalism. Editors Lehóczky and Welsch unite non-UK-born UK-based poets in a celebration of "shared foreignness" including Mimi Khalvati, Jane Yeh, George Szirtes and emerging new voices. Each diverse piece forges a poety of "radical empathy", a defiant poetic community against the darker politics at play in the world today.

BOILER HOUSE PRESS | £15.99 | PBS PRICE £12

## BEOWULF: TRANSLATED BY CHRIS McCULLY

McCully's strong translation of this epic is driven forwards with alliterative, rhythmic tenacity, evoking the rushing of waves, the pulse of battle and the drumming progression of time. This classic legend is rendered in clear but powerful verse, bringing its setting to life in all its beauty and brutality. McCully has himself "unlocked / the sound store of his subtle word-hoard". This text is accompanied by thorough notes on the material and details of creative decisions made in the translation process.

CARCANET | £14.99 | PBS PRICE £11.25

## THE WORLD SPEAKING BACK: TO DENISE RILEY
### EDITED BY ÁGNES LEHÓCZKY AND ZOË SKOULDING

This ambitious anthology marks a "notable birthday" and the major achievements of the distinguished poet and feminist Denise Riley. In this "collective gift" ninety four poets enter into dialogue with and pay living tribute to Riley's poetry, whilst, at the same time, acknowledging the complexity of such a concept. This cross-generational celebration of Riley's multifaceted oeuvre is ideal for the intellectually curious as well as dedicated Riley-readers.

BOILER HOUSE PRESS | £10.00 | PBS PRICE £7.50

## KATE TEMPEST: RUNNING UPON THE WIRES

"My body was like a harp and her words and gestures were like fingers running upon the wires" - James Joyce, *Dubliners*

Powerful, lyrical and rhythmic, Tempest applies her direct and uncompromising vision to matters of the heart. Starting with The End and ending at The Beginning, Tempest tracks the emotional struggle from a relationship break-up, the half-way period when the heart is tugged in two directions to the joy of new love. It is unflinching, raw and painfully honest in the journey it portrays.

PICADOR | £9.99 | PBS PRICE £7.50

BOOK REVIEWS

# PAMPHLETS

## ────── IN THE EMPIRE OF CHIMERAS: MARTIN ANDERSON ──────

Anderson revisits and reworks his poetry of South-East Asia in this enthralling pamphlet. In his opening poem, 'De las Islas e Indios', the poet inhabits the voice of colonised descendants seeing the island habitat slowly destroying colonial architecture: "in the sea wind their basilicas rot." Anderson's precise and evocative environmental description continues throughout, exploring the significance of spaces, how they change, and their representative power.

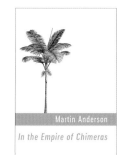

SHEARSMAN | £6.50 |

## ────── THE WARD: LOUISA CAMPBELL ──────

Campbell populates both sides of the mental health ward with a host of vividly drawn characters. Their lives, troubles, diagnoses and treatments are presented in clear, elegant verse. This confident pamphlet navigates questions about mental health with a striking focus on the inherent (and too often forgotten) humanity of its subjects.

PAPER SWANS | £5 |

## ────── INDIFFERENT CRESSES: HOLLY CORFIELD CARR ──────

This finely crafted pamphlet marks the poet's residency at Tyntesfield as part of the National Trust's Women and Power programme. The title is inspired by the 19th Century poet Hannah More who suggested that male readers dismiss women's writing as mere "salad". A suite of wry and knowledgeable prose-poems-as-field-notes accompanied by intriguing and evocative verse, this beautiful book also includes pressed images of botanical subjects and pockets for your own findings.

NATIONAL TRUST | £8 |

## OEDIPA: AMY McCAULEY

This unique work, part poetry pamphlet and part play, is a strange and dizzying rewrite of the Oedipus myth. McCauley's preface warns: "*Oedipa* is a machine which uses the page as its performance space. The voices and stage directions are to be taken literally, which is to say the poem's metaphorical value is nil." Purposefully disorientating and highly intriguing, this unclassifiable work makes its way subversively through themes of mental health, psychoanalysis, critical theory and gender.

GUILLEMOT    PRESS        |        £10        |

## THREADS: SANDEEP PARMAR, NISHA RAMAYYA, BHANU KAPIL

Sandeep Parmar, Nisha Ramayya and Bhanu Kapil innovatively interweave essays, poetry and prose in this thought-provoking exploration of race, self and writing. Parmar explores the nomadic subject, Ramayya proposes a Tantric Poetics and Kapil presents fourteen notes on race. *Threads* raises important questions about subjectivity, representation and challenges how poets of colour can embody the predominantly white male "I" of lyric poetry. Profits go towards the Manuel Bravo Project.

**THREADS**

SANDEEP PARMAR,
NISHA RAMAYYA, BHANU KAPIL

CLINIC            |            £5            |

## NOW THE ROBIN: HAMISH WHYTE

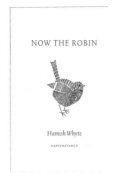

NOW THE ROBIN

Hamish Whyte

HAPPENSTANCE

As summer drifts into autumn, Hamish Whyte welcomes us into his garden where we are gently introduced to birds, trees, flowers and bees. Hamish shares a heartwarming affinity with his garden, giving voice to Robins, as we are treated to his contemplative and comforting observations. Written with apparent simplicity, the poems in this pamphlet leave you with a sense of great contentment and a need to absorb garden-life.

HAPPENSTANCE            |            £5            |

# Poetry Book Society & mslexia

## WOMEN'S POETRY & PAMPHLET COMPETITIONS

WWW.POETRYBOOKS.CO.UK/COMPETITIONS

**POETRY JUDGE: CAROL ANN DUFF**

1st prize: £2000 | 2nd Prize: £400 | 3rd Prize: £200 | Special Prize: £500

**PAMPHLET JUDGE: AMY WACK**

Winner's pamphlet published by Seren Books

DEADLINE 14TH SEPTEMB

# AUTUMN LISTINGS

## NEW BOOKS

| AUTHOR | TITLE | PUBLISHER | RRP |
|---|---|---|---|
| Nick Ascroft | Dandy Bogan: Selected Poems | Boatwhistle Books | £10.00 |
| Sohini Basak | we live in the newness of small differences | Eyewear Publishing | £10.99 |
| Suzanne Batty | States of Happiness | Bloodaxe Books | £9.95 |
| Mara Bergman | The Disappearing Room | Arc Publications | £9.99 |
| Beverley Bie Brahic | The Hotel Eden | Carcanet Press | £9.99 |
| Sophia Blackwell | The Other Woman | Burning Eye Books | £9.99 |
| AK Blakemore | Fondue | Offord Road Books | £10.00 |
| Rachel Bower | Moon Milk | Valley Press | £7.99 |
| Penny Boxall | Who Goes There? | Valley Press | £8.99 |
| Penny Boxall | Ship of the Line | Valley Press | £10.99 |
| Marianne Burton | Kierkegaard's Cupboard | Seren | £9.99 |
| Prudence Bussey-Chamberlain | Coteries | Knives Forks and Spoons | £8.00 |
| Helen Calcutt | Unable Mother | V. Press | £9.99 |
| David Calcutt | The last of the light is not the last of the light | Fair Acre Press | £9.99 |
| Arnaldo Calveyra | Letters So That Happiness | Ugly Duckling Presse | £10.00 |
| Ross Cogan | Bragr | Seren | £9.99 |
| Robert Crawford | The Scottish Ambassador | Jonathan Cape | £10.00 |
| Fred D'Aguiar | Translations From Memory | Carcanet Press | £12.99 |
| Colin Dardis | the x of y | Eyewear Publishing | £10.99 |
| Kwame Dawes and John Kinsella | A New Beginning | Peepal Tree Press | £10.99 |
| Isobel Dixon | The Tempest Prognosticator | Nine Arches Press | £9.99 |
| Isobel Dixon | A Fold in the Map | Nine Arches Press | £9.99 |
| Finuala Dowling | Pretend You Don't Know Me: New and Selected Poems | Bloodaxe Books | £12.00 |
| Afshan D'souza-Lodhi | on desire | Eyewear Publishing | £10.99 |
| Neil Elder | The Space Between Us | Cinnamon Press | £8.99 |
| Kit Fan | As Slow As Possible | Arc Publications | £9.99 |
| Gabriel Fitzmaurice | Will You Be My Friend? | Salmon Poetry | £12.00 |
| John Froy | Sandpaper & Seahorses | Two Rivers Press | £9.99 |
| Iain Galbraith | The True Height of the Ear | Arc Publications | £9.99 |
| Thommie Gillow and Hannah Teasdale | Milked | Burning Eye Books | £9.99 |
| Jess Green | A Self Help Guide to Being in Love with Jeremy Corbyn | Burning Eye Books | £9.99 |
| Jim Greenhalf | Breakfast at Wetherspoons | Smokestack Books | £7.99 |
| Nicki Griffin | Crossing Places | Salmon Poetry | £10.00 |
| Ellen Hinsey | The Illegal Age | Arc Publications | £10.99 |
| Michael Hofmann | One Lark, One Horse | Faber & Faber | £14.99 |
| Gaia Holmes | Where the Road Runs Out | Comma Press | £9.99 |
| Clive James | The River in the Sky | Pan Macmillan | £14.99 |
| Thomas Kabdebo | Ultima Ora | Salmon Poetry | £10.00 |
| Irene Koronas | Ninth Iota | Knives Forks and Spoons | £10.00 |
| Zaffar Kunial | Us | Faber & Faber | £10.99 |
| Frank Kuppner | The Third Mandarin | Carcanet Press | £12.99 |
| Nick Laird | Feel Free | Faber & Faber | £14.99 |
| Ágnes Lehóczky (ed.) | The World Speaking Back to Denise Riley | Boiler House Press | £12.99 |

# AUTUMN LISTINGS

| AUTHOR | TITLE | PUBLISHER | RRP |
|---|---|---|---|
| Ágnes Lehóczky & JT Welsch (eds.) | Wretched Strangers | Boiler House Press | £15.99 |
| Gabriel Levin | Errant | Carcanet Press | £9.99 |
| Richie McCaffery | Passport | Nine Arches Press | £9.99 |
| Neil McCarthy | Stopgap Grace | Salmon Poetry | £10.00 |
| Andrew McMillan | Playtime | Jonathan Cape | £10.00 |
| Brian Meeks | The Coup Clock Ticks | Peepal Tree Press | £9.99 |
| Fiona Moore | The Distal Point | HappenStance Press | £10.00 |
| Benjamin Myers | Heathcliff Adrift | Mayfly Press | £7.99 |
| Ruth Padel | Emerald | Chatto & Windus | £10.00 |
| Robert Peake | Cyclone | Nine Arches Press | £9.99 |
| C. Perricone | Footnotes | Boatwhistle Books | £10.00 |
| Kate Potts | Feral | Bloodaxe Books | £9.95 |
| Cherry Potts (ed.) | Vindication: Poems from Six Women Poets | Arachne Press | £8.99 |
| Lola Ridge, Daniel Tobin (ed.) | To the Many: Collected Early Poems | Little Island Press | £14.00 |
| Miles Salter | The Border | Valley Press | £9.99 |
| Fiona Sinclair | Slow Burner | Smokestack Books | £7.99 |
| Matthew Sweeney | King of a Rainy Country | Arc Publications | £10.99 |
| Kate Tempest | Running Upon The Wires | Picador | £9.99 |
| Jack Thacker | Handling | Two Rivers Press | £8.99 |
| Julian Turner | Desolate Market | Carcanet Press | £9.99 |
| Scott Tyrrell | Honest | Burning Eye Books | £9.99 |
| Anna Vaught | The Life of Almost | Patrician Press | £9.00 |
| Isadora Vibes | soak | Burning Eye Books | £9.99 |
| Chris Wallace-Crabbe | Rondo | Carcanet Press | £9.99 |
| Gordon Walmsley | The Braille of the Sea | Salmon Poetry | £10.00 |
| Tony Walsh | WORK \| LIFE \| BALANCE | Burning Eye Books | £9.99 |
| Mike Watts | Spit and Hiss | Wrecking Ball Press | £10.00 |

## TRANSLATIONS

| AUTHOR | TITLE | PUBLISHER | RRP |
|---|---|---|---|
| José Manuel Cardona, trans. Hélène Cardona | Birnam Wood/El Bosque de Birnam | Salmon Poetry | £10.00 |
| Jure Detela, trans. Raymond Miller & Tatjana Jamnik | Moss & Silver | Ugly Duckling Presse | £14.00 |
| Nora Gomringer, trans. Annie Rutherford | Hydra's Heads | Burning Eye Books | £9.99 |
| Hafez, trans. Mario Petrucci | Beloved: 81 poems from Hafez | Bloodaxe Books | £12.00 |
| Christine Marendon, trans. Ken Cockburn | Heroines from Abroad | Carcanet Press | £12.99 |
| Chris McCully, trans. | Beowulf | Carcanet Press | £14.99 |
| Kristín Ómarsdóttir, trans. Vala Thorodds | Waitress in Fall: Selected Poems | Carcanet Press | £12.99 |
| Kevin M. F. Platt | Orbita: The Project | Arc Publications | £11.99 |
| Sextus Propertius, trans. Patrick Worsnip | Poems | Carcanet Press | £12.99 |
| F Starik and Maarten Inghels, trans. David Colmer et al | Lonely Funeral | Arc Publications | £11.99 |

# PAMPHLETS

| AUTHOR | TITLE | PUBLISHER | RRP |
|---|---|---|---|
| Martin Anderson | In the Empire of Chimeras | Shearsman Books | £6.50 |
| Ian Burnette | Wax | Smith\|Doorstop | £5.00 |
| Louisa Campbell | The Ward | Paper Swans Press | £5.00 |
| Geraldine Clarkson | No. 25 | Shearsman Books | £6.50 |
| James Coghill | Anteater | Eyewear | £6.00 |
| Holly Corfield Carr | Indifferent Cresses | National Trust | £8.00 |
| Beth Dufford | Microscopic Peaceful Implosions | Eyewear | £6.00 |
| Steve Ely | Jubilate Messi | Shearsman Books | £6.50 |
| Brett Evans | Sloth and the Art of Self-deprecation | Indigo Dreams | £6.00 |
| Sarah Fletcher | Typhoid August | Smith\|Doorstop | £5.00 |
| John Foggin | Advice To A Traveller | Indigo Dreams | £6.00 |
| Miriam Gordis | Vinyl | Eyewear | £6.00 |
| Michael Grieve | Luck | HappenStance Press | £3.00 |
| Lizzi Hawkins | Osteology | Smith\|Doorstop | £5.00 |
| Selima Hill | Fishtank | Flarestack | £6.00 |
| Stefan Kielbasiewicz | Stealing Shadow | Smith\|Doorstop | £5.00 |
| Joan Lennon | GRANNY GARBAGE | HappenStance Press | £3.00 |
| Holly Magill | The Becoming of Lady Flambé | Indigo Dreams | £6.00 |
| Sean Magnus Martin | Flood-Junk | Against the Grain | £5.00 |
| Amy McCauley | Oedipa | Guillemot Press | £10.00 |
| Gerry Murphy | My Life as a Stalinist | Southword Editions | £4.99 |
| James O'Leary | There are Monsters in this House | Southword Editions | £4.99 |
| Sandeep Parmar, Bhanu Kapil & Nisha Ramayya | Threads | clinic | £5.99 |
| Simon Perril | In the Final Year of My 40s | Shearsman Books | £6.50 |
| Jenna Plewes | Against the Pull of Time | V. Press | £6.50 |
| Christian Wethered | I Don't Love You | Eyewear | £6.00 |
| Hamish Whyte | NOW THE ROBIN | HappenStance Press | £5.00 |